INTRODUCTION

Working with young people for several years has left me with countless stories and numerous laughs. While ordering "chicken nibblets" at McDonalds or trying to sneak into the play place may be harmless pranks, a lot of young people make choices with much greater consequences. I'm going to be honest with you, young people are dumb (I'm including my age group as well). If you don't believe me, then look at the young people around you. There are examples everywhere. I don't want to be like them and I don't wan't you to be like them either. How can we avoid falling into such foolishness that ruins young lives all around us? How can we be wise beyond our years? The answer is by learning God's Word and applying it to our lives.

Proverbs is known as the book of wisdom. In God's perfect knowledge He used a king named Solomon, who made many foolish decisions, to write a book on what to do and what not to do. Everything Solomon writes he learned from experience. The purpose of this book is to give moral instruction, especially to young people. Proverbs 1:1-4 says "The proverbs of Solomon the son of David, king of Israel. To know wisdom and instruction; to perceive the words of understanding; to receive the instructions of wisdom, justice, and judgement, and equity; to give subtilty to the simple, to the young man knowledge and discretion." If you want to be different than those around you and make better choices in your life, then read the book of Proverbs and listen to what the Word of God has to say. This daily devotional will help you dive into the Word of God and allow it to shape and mold you into being the person that God wants you to be. I encourage you to spend time with God throughout this book and allow Him and His Word to influence all of your life decisions. I promise you won't regret it! Let's get started!

Day 1
Student or Fool?
Scripture Reading: Proverbs 1:1-7

Notice the word "simple" and the phrase "young man" in verse 4. "Simple" refers to one who is easily led to either good or evil. We are a simple people. We are easily led to believe certain philosophies, do certain things, and live certain lives. The phrase "young man" refers to those who are inexperienced. Young people are both inexperienced and easily led. Your need for the book of Proverbs is greater than you think! Just look at the people in your school. If teenagers weren't easily influenced then Kanye West wouldn't have a clothing line. Can you see how easily our generation is influenced by athletes, celebrities, popular kids, etc.? However, being easily influenced isn't necessarily a bad thing. It also means that you can be easily influenced by the Word of God.

Verse 5 tells us what wise people do. First of all, they listen. How many young people hear the Word of God being taught and simply block it out of their minds? They discredit it as if it's dumb and insignificant. But the wise will listen and apply the truths to their lives. For example, if my doctor said that I'm allergic to peanuts and that by eating one I could die, then I would have two choices. I could either be wise and listen to what he had to say by avoiding peanuts, or I could say, "whatever, a peanut couldn't hurt me. He doesn't know what he's talking about," and then proceed to eat a peanut and have a deadly reaction. God's Word is very similar. We can either listen to it and apply it to our lives (the wise

4

option), or say "whatever" and do things our way (the deadly option).

In verse 7 the Bible says, "the fear of the Lord is beginning of knowledge." To fear God isn't to be afraid of Him. It is to reverence His power and authority. Knowledge begins when we understand that God is the Creator of the universe and is the ultimate authority in our lives. Wisdom is to recognize that He knows what is best for our lives and the Bible is His instruction book to us. It is therefore wise if we read it, listen to it, and obey it. Fools, on the other hand, hate wisdom. They want nothing to do with God's Word and what it has to say. They call it "stupid, dumb, and outdated." What are you going to be: A student of God's Word or a fool?

- How can the fact that you are easily influenced be a good thing?
- What steps will you take to be wise?
- Are you acknowledging God as the ultimate authority in your life?

Prayer: Lord, in a world of so many ideas and philosophies, help me to learn the truth from Your Word. Influence me each day as I spend time in my daily devotions. Teach me Your truths and help me apply them to my life.

DAY 2
BETTER THAN BLING
Scripture Reading: Proverbs 1:8-9

Athletes will do almost anything to win a championship ring. Before Lebron James ever won a championship (the good ole days), there was a Nike commercial featuring puppets of Lebron James and Kobe Bryant. In these commercials, Kobe would usually make fun of Lebron for not having any rings. In sports, you could have the best stats in the world, set all the records, but you are not validated until you have that precious championship ring. That's why athletes work so hard to get better and stay in shape. To most athletes, the ring is everything.

In this passage, the Bible compares the instructions of godly parents to that of a high and honorable reward made of gold. Do you understand what the Bible is saying? That the instruction of godly parents is better than a Super Bowl ring! But often times we view their instructions as "unfair," "old fashioned," and "dumb." I understand it's not always easy to listen to our parents. There's been plenty of times in my life where I didn't agree with them, but in those times I am either glad I listened, or wish I had.

Pay attention to the words "hear," and "forsake not." You are human. Therefore you are not always going to want to hear what your parents have to say, let alone do what they say. There will be numerous times when you will be tempted to "forsake" the instructions of your parents. Our culture even promotes rebelling against your parents, but God's way is best. Your parents have something better than a championship ring: godly instruction. I promise you will never regret listening and not forsaking their instruction.

   I understand that not everyone has godly parents. If that's you, it's okay! While we should still follow God's Word and respect them, we should seek wise counsel from godly figures in our lives such as pastors, youth pastors, teachers, or people in the church. Allow these people to help influence you in all areas of life. Their instruction is precious!

- How much influence do you allow your parents/ godly figures to have in your life?
- Are you allowing your parents/godly figures to help direct you in who you should date, where you should go to school, career choices, etc.? Hint: You should!

Prayer: Lord, thank You for the godly influences You have placed in my life. Help me to listen and apply their instruction even when I don't want to. By doing so, I trust that You know what is best for my life.

DAY 3
DON'T FALL FOR IT
Scripture Reading: Proverbs 1:10-19

Have you ever been persuaded to do something that you regretted? As a teenager, my friend invited me and someone else to spend the night at his house. They were both good friends of mine so I quickly accepted the invite. In my mind, I was sure it would be a good time. I could just see us eating junk food, playing video games, watching movies. What could possibly go wrong? I arrived at his house and immediately started having an allergic reaction to his cat. But I decided that a little sneezing and runny nose wasn't going to stop me from enjoying myself. Not long after that, I sat on his couch only to find half eaten corn dogs poking out of the cushions, along with other foods that were too decayed to identify. Again, I tried to push through and have a good time. But later that night, as I laid on the floor trying to go to sleep, my allergies were so bad that it caused my asthma to flare up. It was at that point, lying in the cat hair infested floor, that I wished I would have stayed home. I wish I would have never accepted this invitation. I was completely miserable and the consequences of going seemed unbearable.

In Proverbs 1:10-19 we see a similar scenario of what happens when we say "yes" to the evil invitation of ungodly people. Just like I wished I wouldn't have accepted my invitation to sleep over at my friends house, those who accept this evil invitation will regret their decision as well. Only their consequences will be much more serious and painful.

This passage talks about the invitation of sinners. No one likes to sin alone. Sinners will do their best to get you to join them. That's why gangs are so prevalent in our society. The Bible even calls this invitation "enticing." That word means attractive or tempting. There's a reason why so many young people get involved in sin: because it offers pleasure. In verse 13, the Bible says sinners will entice you by saying, "we shall find all precious substance, we shall fill our houses with spoil." This is one of the devil's greatest lies. He makes many promises of rewards and pleasure, but the rewards are anything but great. The point is, sinners aren't satisfied in sinning alone. They want you to join them. Your classmates want you to join them in doing drugs and alcohol. Your friends don't want to be the only one listening to ungodly music. They want someone to join them in their perverted jokes, impure relationships, bullying, thievery, and so on. Therefore, they will do their best to persuade you to join them as they offer pleasure and great rewards. And because you are young and inexperienced, you may be tempted to join them. So what should we do?

Verse 10 says when sinners try and persuade you to join them "consent not." That simply means do not accept! God's Word gives us two extremely helpful commands in verse 15. The first one is "walk not thou in the way with them." This means to avoid companionship with bad influences. One of the most dangerous things you can do as a young person is have close relationships with ungodly people. There's nothing wrong with being friendly to the ungodly. Jesus was even friendly with sinners. But we should never have close relationships with them because sooner or later we will end up joining them in their sinful quest.

Secondly, God's Word instructs us to "refrain thy foot from their path." I've heard young people say, "yeah, I go to parties with drinking and drugs but I don't ever do them." By saying this they are telling me that it's okay to be with them as long as they don't partake in their sin. That's foolishness! That's walking in their path. When you walk in the paths of evil, you will eventually fail to resist the temptation and partake in the sin it offers. Bad company will lead you to bad conduct just as a sinful path will lead you to sin. The only way to guarantee safety is to stay away from both.

What kind of friends do you have? Are your close relationships ones that persuade you to live for God or tempt you to sin? Do you put yourself in places where sinful things are taking place or where wholesome things are happening? It's either one or the other. Commentator Albert Barnes says, "the first great danger which besets the simple and the young is that of evil companionship. The only safety is to be found in the power of saying 'No', to all such invitations."[1]

---

[1]Barnes, Albert, H. C. Leupold, and Robert Frew. Barnes' Notes on the Old and New Testaments: A Practical and Explanatory Commentary. Grand Rapids, MI: Baker Book House, 1949. Print.

One of the very first things king Solomon talks about is staying away from bad influences. God knew just how important it was for young people to hear that.

- Are there any bad influences or friendships that you need to get rid of?
- What do you need to do in order to "refrain from their path?"
- What other things did God speak to your heart about when reading this passage?

Prayer: Lord, help me to stay away from bad influences. If there are any relationships that I need to change then give me the courage to do so. May they understand the reason I cannot hang out with them and may You use that to work in their heart.

Pray for:

Steve Redman   Robin Johnson.

Jim Banunam

Carl Night

Matt Hickey

Luke Robertson

Anthony Marcus

Derick Webb

DAY 4
CONSEQUENCES OF REJECTING WISDOM
Scripture Reading: Proverbs 1:20-33

My wife is notorious for losing her phone. Looking for her phone is a daily routine in our household. She usually says something like "Trav, where is my phone. I seriously can't find it anywhere." And then I'll usually resolve the matter by saying "it's in your purse," or "you're sitting on it!" Most of the time, it is right in front of her face! Yet, she doesn't see it. Wisdom is a lot like that. The Bible says "wisdom crieth out." That word carries the idea of shouting. The fact is, wisdom doesn't hide itself. It's not something that you have to search for and find. It's literally right in front of your face! God's Word is so clear about what we should and shouldn't do. The fact that you are reading this book proves that wisdom is literally right in front of your face! But what will you do with it?

Read verses 24-25 again. God is saying, "I have given you wisdom. I have given you every opportunity to know what is right and to do it. But you chose not to listen." As a young man or woman, you have so many opportunities to be different than those around you and choose wisdom. And if you're reading this book then someone obviously cares enough about you to help you learn and know wisdom. God has given you every opportunity to know what is wise and how to apply it. By not choosing wisdom, you're not only being foolish, but you are openly rejecting God. That's a scary place to be.

So what happens when you reject God's wisdom? Verses 26-31 paint us a clear picture and it's not a pretty one. When you reject God's wisdom there will always be consequences. You reap what you sow. Look at some of things people reap when they reject God. This passage uses words such as fear, desolation, destruction, and anguish. Rejecting wisdom will bring you emotional, physical, and spiritual pain. In other words, it's never worth it. Ever.

Thankfully, this passage ends with a wonderful promise to those who take God's wisdom and live by it. Verse 33 says those people will "dwell safely," and avoid "fear of evil." The way of the fool is hard. It's full of fear, uncertainty, and problems. But the ways of God offer safety and freedom from fear. The word "safely" carries the idea of being confident and secure as you rest in the promises of a loving God[2]. The freedom of fear is something the wicked know nothing of for they are in constant anxiety of being caught by parents or police. Fearing the people they have done wrong will get revenge. There is no peace or safety for the fool. Only those who do things God's way have such peace.

- What has God spoken to your heart about as you read His Word?
- God has given you the opportunity to learn and know wisdom. Are you applying it to your life?
- Do you know anyone who has rejected God's wisdom? How has his or her life turned out?

[2]"Overview - English Annotations on the Holy Bible." *StudyLight.org*. N.p., n.d. Web. 05 May 2017.

- Do you know anyone who has followed God's wisdom? How has his or her life turned out so far?

Prayer: Lord, thank You for making your wisdom so clear to me. Help, me to apply it to my life. Remind me of the consequences of rejecting wisdom along with the benefits of following Your instructions.

Day 5
THERE'S SAFETY IN WISDOM
Scripture Reading: Proverbs 2

Reading the first 9 verses of this passage we see a wonderful promise to those who seek after wisdom. God promises that if we seek wisdom, He will give it to us. After all, He wants us to have wisdom! One of the most important things you can do is seek the wisdom of the Omniscient (all-knowing) God. In the rest of this chapter, we learn of the benefits God's wisdom gives us.

During the initial construction of the Golden Gate Bridge in San Francisco, California, no safety devices were used. People working on the bridge had neither a harness to keep them from falling, nor a net to protect them if they did fall. As a result, 23 men fell off the bridge and died while working. After the 23rd death, they finally put a safety net at the bottom which saved at least 10 lives.[3]

It's very easy to look back and call them foolish for not having a safety net at the beginning, or at least after the first man died. But in reality, it took 23 men falling to their deaths to get them to realize the necessity of a net. In this passage, the Bible illustrates wisdom as a safety net. Going through life (especially young adulthood) without God's wisdom is like working on the Golden Gate Bridge without a safety net.

[3]*StudyLight.org*. N.p., n.d. Web. 09 May 2017.

15

There are three words in verses 11-12 that I want you to notice. The words "preserve," "keep," and "deliver" all have something in common: they protect us! The word "preserve" carries the idea of a watchman or guard warning us when danger is near. "Keep" implies strong protection like a wall that keeps the intrusion of evil out. And "deliver" suggests the idea of rescuing us from danger.[4] Can you see how critical it is to follow God's Word?

So what exactly does wisdom protect us from? There are obviously many things, but this passage focuses on two: bad influences, and perverted relationships. Since we have already covered the importance of keeping good company in previous chapters, we're going to focus on how wisdom can keep us from devastating relationships. Read verses 16-19 again. Notice the phrase "strange woman." The Bible uses that phrase to describe a prostitute. And although it is referring to a woman here, the same can be applied the other way around. The Bible describes this person with 4 phrases. The first one is "she flattereth with her words." This person is seductive, tempting, and will do anything to "talk you into it." Next, the Bible says "she forsaketh the guide of her youth," which means she is rebellious toward her parents and authority. The phrase "she forgetteth the covenant of her God" indicates her rejection of God's Word. And lastly the Bible says her ways "lead to death," which implies her lifestyle of sin brings about ruin.

[4]Butler, John G. *Proverbs to Song of Solomon*. Clinton, IA: LBC Publications, 2013. Print.

After we have looked at this person we would be a fool for wanting a relationship with anyone like him or her. However, without the wisdom of God, we could very easily find ourselves involved in such relationships. People like that seem harmless at first, but they slowly lure you in and before you know it that relationship has ruined so many parts of your life. So instead of falling for someone like that, rely on God's wisdom to keep you safe from such relationships and wait on the Lord to bring you someone the complete opposite. Someone who isn't seductive in their dress, words, or lifestyle. Someone who respects his or her parents and authority. And someone who is dedicated to following the ways of God. Do this and you won't ruin your life like so many young people have already done.

When Jim Elliot, the great missionary to Ecuador, was in college he was known as a "woman hater." Not because he necessarily hated women, but because he thought that it was a waste of time and very dangerous to get involved in a relationship when it wasn't necessary. Instead of trying helplessly to find a spouse, like so many people do, he simply waited on God. In one of his letters Jim wrote, "No one warns young people to follow Adam's example. He waited till God saw his need. Then God made Adam sleep, prepared for his mate, and brought her to him."[5]

---

[5]Elliot, Elisabeth. Shadow of the Almighty: The Life & Testament of Jim Elliot. San Francisco: Harper & Row, 1989. Print.

What great advice! God knows what we need and He is faithful to always give us what we need. A spouse is no different. Trust that God will give you someone to marry and in the meantime stay clear of those relationships that will lead to heartache and ruin.

- Are there any relationships that you need to get rid of?
- What have you learned about the type of person you should look for in a spouse?
- What else has God spoken to your heart about while reading this passage?

Prayer: Lord, thank You for giving me wisdom when I ask for it and seek it. Help me to rely on Your wisdom in all of our decisions. May I use Your wisdom to protect me from bad relationships.

DAY 6
DON'T TRUST YOURSELF
Scripture Reading: Proverbs 3:1-6

Once again we see the blessings of knowing God's wisdom and applying it to our lives in the first 4 verses of this passage. Verse 2 promises length of days and peace. Although everyone is susceptible to tragic accidents and sickness, those who live right usually live longer than those who do not. Think of all the people who die early because of drugs, alcohol, smoking, etc. Another promise this passage gives is of peace. What good is it to accomplish so much during the day only to toss and turn at night because you have no peace? Right living gives peace. Lastly, verse 4 promises favor from God and man. Those who live according to the scripture are usually well liked. And who wouldn't want the favor of God in their lives?

Today, we're going to focus on one of the most popular verses in all of Scripture: Proverbs 3:5-6. After graduating high school my grandpa, who was also my pastor at the time, gave me a study Bible. In it he wrote, "trust in the Lord with all thine heart; and lean not unto thine own understanding. In all thy ways acknowledge him, and he shall direct thy paths." Little did I know just how significant those two verses would be to me in the next few years.

As a senior at Southeastern Free Will Baptist College, I was preparing to get married to my then fiancée, and trying to figure out where God wanted me to serve the following year. That definitely made for an interesting two semesters. My fiancée and I often disagreed on what we would do after college. I wanted to go wherever God led, which I thought might be my hometown in Michigan, and she wanted to stay closer to her parents in North Carolina. I had some big decisions to make and wasn't sure what to do. Half way through my last semester I went to my favorite restaurant, Grand Street Pizza, for lunch after church. While eating a delicious slice of pizza, I received a text message from my fiancée saying, "we need to talk." If you have ever been in a relationship, then you know those words are usually a bad sign. I knew it was bad news, but there was no way I was about to ruin my lunch by replying. I was going to enjoy every bite of pizza before I dealt with that text. Towards the end of lunch, I started scrolling on Facebook and came across a devotion that one of my friends had posted. The writer talked about trusting God even when it didn't make sense. Even when it was scary. And he referred to Proverbs 3:5-6. At that point, I knew that it was God's will for me to go serve at Faith Free Will Baptist Church in Michigan.

"Trust in the Lord with all thine heart" is a command to place your trust in Him and not in things, people, or finances. My then fiancée was worried about money, seeing her family, etc. And to be honest, the money wasn't there. I didn't know how it would work. But we are to trust in God, the Giver of all things good. The faithful God who will always give us what's best. The God who promises to always meet our needs. We are to trust in Him and not ourselves. The phrase "lean not," carries the idea of resting. So many people rest and rely on good jobs with great money, comfortable houses, or their plan for their lives. But the Bible says to trust God, rest upon Him, and not your own understanding of what you think is best.

Verse 6 says, "in all thy ways acknowledge him, and he shall direct thy paths." If you're wise, then you want God to direct your paths. That's what made that decision in college so difficult. I wanted so badly to do what God wanted me to do. But how could I know what that was? The Bible gives a simple formula. We can know His path by acknowledging Him in all things. We can do that by simply praying, "God what would you have me to do here?" One professor told me, "ask God to make it clear and He will." That's exactly what I did. I prayed and waited on God to make it extremely clear and He did just that! In fact, He answered my prayers in ways far greater than I expected. His path for me was totally different than the one I had planned, and I'm so grateful for that! Instead of marrying my then fiancée, God broke us up because He had someone better for me waiting at the church where I would serve in Michigan after graduation. She's the most beautiful, wonderful wife that I ever could have dreamed of. Only God could do that. Trusting in God and seeking his direction is worth it. It has definitely paid off in my life!

Young people, I encourage you to trust in the Lord. I know we all have ideas of what we want our lives to be like, of who we want to marry, what kind of careers we want, etc. But God's paths are different than ours. And even when it's hard to trust Him, trust Him anyways knowing that His path is far greater than the one you're dreaming of.

- What has God taught you in this passage?

- Why do so many people trust in themselves rather than God?
- What steps will you take right now in order to let God direct your paths? Hint: prayer, godly counsel, and Bible reading!

Prayer: Lord, I'm so grateful that You are a faithful God who wants what's best for my life. I pray that You would direct my life. Sometimes our understanding tells us one thing while Yours is saying another. Help me to trust You and not myself because Your ways are always best.

DAY 7
IT PAYS TO GIVE
Scripture Reading: Proverbs 3:9-10

Giving isn't something that always comes easy for us. We see it in children who refuse to give someone else their toy. We see it in people who hoard their money and refuse to spend a dime. I even see it in myself when my wife doesn't order fries and then asks if she can have some of mine. The point is, it's not always natural to give. But if you start giving while you're young it will become a habit that will change your life for the better.

We know we are to honor our Lord with our lives, bodies, time, and possessions. But we often fail to realize that we are to honor the Lord with our substance. When the Bible uses the word "substance" it is referring to the material things we gain. We often apply this to our money knowing that God's Word tells us to give at least ten percent of what we earn back to the Lord. After all, without His provision in our lives we wouldn't have anything to give in the first place. However, substance can also apply to the things we have such as cars, property, etc. In college there were many students who didn't have a vehicle. I would often let them borrow my car or drive them places myself. My thinking was that God has given me this car so I'm going to use it to give back. We should all plan on giving back what God has given us.

Does anyone like leftovers? Even if you do, odds are you like the food better when it is fresh. There are many issues with leftovers; a few of them stick in my mind. First of all, leftovers don't taste that great. They may taste good, but never as good as they once were. Secondly, there's usually not a lot of leftovers which leaves you hungry and unsatisfied. Lastly, sometimes leftovers get eaten by someone else. If you live in my house, I give you one day to eat your leftovers. After that, it's free game. The fact is, leftovers aren't great and most of the time there isn't much left over at all. The Bible says to "Honor the Lord with thy substance and with the first fruits of all thine increase." God deserves our best. Not what's leftover.

The best financial decision you will ever make is to give God ten percent of what you earn. In verse 9 there is a sense of persistency and priority in giving. We should faithfully give God our very best. Giving God ten percent should be our number one financial priority. Don't wait until your bills are paid to see if you have any money left over. Give to God first!

I've heard many people say that they can't afford not to tithe. At first that statement doesn't make any sense. But in reality it couldn't be more accurate. Notice verse 10 of this passage when it talks about what happens when we give. Simply put, God blesses those who honor Him in giving! Regarding those who give, John Gill states, "Instead of having less, they should have abundantly more."[6] You can't out give God! The more you give God the more He gives to you. It's a wonderful cycle! I could copy and paste story after story about people who have gotten out of debt because they started to tithe and give to God. I've never heard of a dedicated tither being in want of anything. God blesses those who honor Him in their giving. John Butler says, "When you give to God faithfully and first, He will see to it that you are adequately taken care of in your needs."[7]

While there are a lot of places you could go to get financial advice, no place is better than God's Word. There are plenty of wise things you can do with your money, but the wisest thing you could do is give it.

- Are you giving God ten percent of everything you earn?
- Are you using the things God has given you to be a blessing to others?
- Are you dedicated to make giving your number one financial priority?

Prayer: Lord, help me to honor You with all the things You have given me. I am going to commit

[6]Gill, John. "Commentary on Proverbs 3:9". "The New John Gill Exposition of the Entire Bible". http://www.studylight.org/commentaries/geb/proverbs-3.html. 1999.

[7]Butler, John G. *Proverbs to Song of Solomon*. Clinton, IA: LBC Publications, 2013. Print.

ten percent of everything I earn to You. By doing
so, I am trusting that You will take care of me and
my needs.

DAY 8
EMBRACE CHASTENING
Scripture Reading: Proverbs 3:11-12

"Chastening" means to correct or discipline. It is something that we all need, but rarely enjoy. We recently put up a fence in our backyard to keep our dog from leaving the yard. To say he's not a fan of the fence is a massive understatement. He absolutely hates it. In fact, within the span of 5 days, he escaped 3 times. Every time we came home to realize he escaped, I tried to make adjustments so he couldn't get out. Finally, when I thought we had completely escape proofed the fence, he dug out. When I got home I couldn't believe it. I sternly disciplined him and then tied him up by the hole he dug hoping to teach him a lesson.

Our dog obviously didn't enjoy it, but it was for his own good. You see, I wasn't attempting to keep him inside the fence because I was keeping him from something good. I was trying to keep him from getting lost or getting hit by a car. The discipline wasn't being done out of cruelty, but out of love and protection. God's Word is like a fence. It doesn't keep us from good things like many people believe. Instead, it keeps us from bad things. And when we break His laws, He chastens (disciplines) us.

While it's natural to hate being disciplined, the Bible says to "Despise not the chastening of the Lord." God chastens us when we sin by making us feel guilty. He brings up the sin to our conscience and it bothers us. No one enjoys that time. I have had many days ruined because of God's correction. But we shouldn't be angry at God for chastening us. Instead, it should make us happy.

Make us happy? That doesn't sound right. In fact, it seems kind of impossible to be happy when you're being chastened by a Holy God. But the Bible gives us good reason in verse 12 when it says "For whom the Lord loveth he correcteth; even as a father the son in whom he delighteth." If you sin and feel the chastening of the Lord then it shows you 2 things: you're saved and God loves you. The reason I disciplined my dog when he dug the hole was because I cared about him. If I didn't like the dog then I wouldn't have cared if he ran off and never came back. My discipline was out of love. God does the same thing when He disciplines us. Don't be mad. Embrace it, knowing that you're a child of the King and that He loves you very much. Hebrews 12:6 says, "For whom the Lord loveth he chasteneth, and scourgeth every son whom he receiveth."

What will you do when God chastens you? Will you try and push it off, acting like it doesn't bother you and rebel against it? Or will you embrace it, knowing that the Lord loves you and it's for your own good?

- How do you respond to God's loving correction?
- Have you ever thanked God for caring enough about you to chasten you when you do wrong?
- What other things has God spoken to your heart about while reading this passage?

28

Prayer: God, thank You for caring so much about me to chasten me. Help me to embrace Your loving correction instead of rebelling against it.

DAY 9
REAL KINDNESS
Scripture Reading: Proverbs 3:13-28

Although we've read quite a few verses from this passage, we're going to focus on verses 27-28. It is in these verses that the Bible talks about what it really means to display kindness. While it is easy to be kind in certain situations, sometimes being kind is costly. It may even mean being kind to someone who is undeserving or unlikeable.

I recently took some teenagers to an event called All Access Days at Southeastern Free Will Baptist College. During the trip, our teenagers got an opportunity to see what it would be like to be college students. On our way down we stayed at a hotel in West Virginia. The next morning, one of our teenagers got the brilliant idea to chuck his bag over the second floor balcony onto the pavement. It didn't seem like a big deal at the time. After all, this was a fairly normal occurrence. However, as he was getting ready for class the next day, he realized his body wash had busted and spilled all over his only pair of pants. Since going to class with no pants was not an option, Josh (who was quite a bit smaller) had an extra pair of pants that he let him wear. Although he was afraid that his pants would get stretched out and not fit him anymore, he still let his friend Lucas wear them. His kindness may have cost him a pair of pants, but he displayed true kindness that this passage of scripture talks about.

Notice the phrase "When it is in the power of thine hand to do it," in verse 27. This talks about the opportunity and ability to display kindness. By having an extra pair of pants, Josh had the opportunity and ability to give Lucas some much needed trousers. The Bible says "withhold not good" when you have the opportunity and ability to be kind. That literally means to be kind every time you can. It is wise to be charitable. Yet many people hold to the "it's your problem, not mine," theory. Don't fall for that thinking!

Verse 28 talks about being quick to act in kindness. Don't delay! If you're in high school or college, it's very likely that you have a close relationship with the word "procrastination." In fact, you may be reading this just so you don't have to start writing a paper or study for a test. It's so easy to procrastinate and put things off. That is also the case with kindness. When Josh had an opportunity to be kind to Lucas, he could have said, "if you're pants don't dry before class starts I'll give you mine," or "if no one else gives you some then you can have mine." Instead of putting off our kindness, we should jump at the opportunity to display kindness!

True, biblical kindness doesn't withhold and it doesn't wait. It jumps at the opportunity to be kind and takes advantage of it. Think of it this way: when you are kind to others you are allowing the kindness of God to be displayed through your life! What a blessing it is be kind to others!

I'm afraid that too often we let the opportunity to be kind slip away because we don't like that person or don't want to give up our time, possessions, or money. We may even limit our kindness to friends and the people we like. The Bible says to be kind to "whom it is due." Since we have an obligation to show the love of God to all men, then everyone falls in to the "whom it is due" category.

- Are you taking advantage of every opportunity you have to be kind?
- Are you being kind to those who aren't your friends such as parents, siblings, or different kids at school?
- Are you wiling to be kind even though it may cost you?
- What else have you learned from reading this passage?

Prayer: Lord, thank You so much for the kindness You have given me. Dying for my sin is the greatest example of love and kindness there could ever be. May Your kindness motivate me to be kind to others. Use my kindness to show others Your unconditional love.

DAY 10
A PACKAGE DEAL
Scripture Reading: Proverbs 3:33-35

Whenever I order a meal at a restaurant it often comes with a salad. I'm not a big salad guy, so I usually just eat the croutons with some ranch and then let someone else eat the rest. It doesn't matter if I want one or not. It always comes with the meal. Similarly, the way you live your life comes as a package deal. The Bible uses three words to describe what you get if you live right (according to His Word), and three words to describe what comes with a sinful life. The words "blessing," "grace," and "glory" accompany those who live right. "Curse," "scorn," and "shame" go with those who live in sin. Whether you want those things or not it doesn't matter. It's a package deal. You can't live right without having God's blessing, grace, and glory rain down on your life. Neither can you live in sin without curse, scorn, and shame following you. It's a package deal.

Verse 33 says "The curse of the Lord is in the house of the wicked." God is a holy God. Many claim that if God was loving and good then He wouldn't punish sin. But in reality, God punishes sin because He is so loving and good. He does this in order to stir them to righteous living and eternal life in Heaven. Would a good cop allow a murderer to go free? Of course not. Therefore, as a good, just, and loving God, He cannot allow sin to go unpunished. As a result, the sinner's house is filled with the punishment of his wrongdoings. On the other hand, the Bible says that those who live right have the blessings of God in their home. What a contrast! Being in ministry, I have the opportunity to get a personal look inside the homes of many people. As a result, I've seen first hand just how true this passage is. People who don't live right usually have pretty rough lives. Their homes are usually a mess. Their family is dysfunctional. There are always problems. Contrarily, the homes of the righteous are filled with joy and blessings from God! Just look around and you will find this to be true.

The word "scorn" refers to the feeling or belief that something is worthless. It can also refer to those who are fighting God's authority. Sinners scorn at God and His Word. They claim that living for Him is worthless and meaningless. In verse 34, we see that God will give the scorners a taste of their own medicine. He will scorn them. While they spend much of their time scorning God and his children, the day will come when they will pay for their actions. Meanwhile, God will "give grace to the lowly." That phrase is referring to those who have been oppressed by scorners. If you have ever been made fun of or criticized for living for God, then this is talking about you. While you have taken a lot of persecution from scorners, God will repay you with His wonderful grace! The very definition of God's grace is receiving something good that we don't deserve. Who wouldn't want God's goodness and favor on his life?

Lastly, the Bible says, "The wise shall inherit glory." People will do almost anything for glory. Athletes work out and practice hard in order to receive glory. Teenagers often do stupid stunts in order to receive glory from their friends. But God's Word says true glory belongs to the wise (those who learn God's Word and do it). While the wise enjoy the blessings and grace of righteous living right away, glory will be theirs once they get to heaven. Don't you want to be a part of that group? Conversely, those who reject God's way of living will receive shame. Wickedness always results in shame. When Adam and Eve sinned one of their first feelings afterward was that of shame. Many people live their lives being ashamed of the things they have done. What a awful way to live life. Future glory is far greater than present shame.

What package deal are you purchasing? Is the way you're living going to produce blessings, grace, and glory? Or will you end up with punishment, scorn, and shame? Being so young, you have the opportunity to make sure your future is filled with the blessings and favor of the Almighty God. God is a good God. One worthy of obeying. May Psalm 84:11 encourage you as it reads "For the Lord God is a sun and shield: the Lord will give grace and glory: no good thing will he withhold from them that walk uprightly."

Maybe you haven't always made the best choices. Maybe there are some things you have done that you're ashamed of. Thankfully, God is a merciful and forgiving God. He wants to forgive you and change your life for the better. If there are things in your life that aren't right with God, I encourage you to repent and ask God to forgive you. Then, you can begin to experience the joy of serving Christ with your life!

- Can you think of someone who's home is filled with sin's punishment as a result of wicked living?

- Can you think of a family who lives for God and is experiencing joy and blessings in their home?
- What do you want your future home to be filled with?
- What did God speak to your heart about while reading this passage?

Prayer: Lord, thank You for Your Word that shows me the right way to live. Help me to remember the joy and blessings of living right as well as the curse and punishment of wicked living. Help me to be wise in my decisions and to live according to Your Word.

DAY 11
HOW TO PROTECT YOUR HEART
Scripture Reading: Proverbs 4

When my wife and I bought our first house we had a little problem with ants. Actually, it was a pretty big problem. They were everywhere! And they were big! You couldn't go to the kitchen without killing two or three ants. They even made their way to our food as my wife was cooking one day and discovered them in the powdered sugar. My wife even had nightmares of ants being in our bed. These ants were having way too much influence on our lives. Something had to be done. So we decided to buy some ant traps and place them by our doors where they were entering. To this day, those traps are still there guarding our home from those terrible ants. If we were to throw out the traps, those ants would be right back. The only way to keep the ants away is to stay on guard!

Read verses 23-27 again. Here the Bible says to guard our hearts. In the Scriptures, the Bible often refers to our will, thoughts, and affection when it uses the word "heart." While most young people take no thought in protecting their hearts, the book of wisdom puts extraordinary value in guarding your heart. Why? "For out of it are the issues of life." You see everything we do or say is first conceived in our heart. If we allow negative influences into our thoughts, will, and affections, then those negative influences will show up in our actions. So what can we do to protect our hearts?

First of all, we are to guard our ears from evil speech. Verse 24 says "Put away from thee a froward mouth, and perverse lips put far from thee." This verse is talking about any type of speech that is perverted, ungodly, inappropriate, etc. It also refers to gossip and speaking bad of others. Oh how easy it is to allow this type of speech to not only enter our ears, but also come out of our mouths. We must first get rid of the evil speech that comes out of our mouths, and then keep ourselves away from people who use such speech the best we can. In order to guard our hearts, we must guard our ears.

Secondly, we must guard our eyes. There's a lot of truth to the children's song that sings "Oh be careful little eyes what you see." In order to keep your heart from evil, we must guard what enters our heart through our eyes. We live in a culture where the lustful eye can always find something immoral to look at. Even scarier, our eyes can often come across evil without even trying. To be honest, it's almost impossible to watch television or go out in public without seeing something inappropriate. We must do all we can to keep our eyes from seeing evil. While keeping evil from entering our eyes is difficult, it helps to focus our eyes on Jesus and His Word.

Lastly, we are to guard our hands and feet. In order to do that, the Bible says to "ponder the path of they feet." That means to deeply consider where your actions will lead you. Will they lead you to good or evil? Before we do anything questionable we should ask ourselves, "Will this lead to good or bad?" Then we should always choose the path that is good.

Your heart is incredibly valuable. Satan knows it and is doing all he can to destroy it. He's got many weapons to attack our ears, eyes, and actions. If we don't guard against these attacks then our hearts will be infiltrated with wickedness. Do you understand just how important it is to guard your heart?

- Are you protecting you ears, eyes, hands and feet from evil?
- What area do you need to work on most?
- What has God specifically spoken to your heart about?

Prayer: Heavenly Father, help me to guard my heart. You know just how difficult it can be to protect myself from evil when it is all around me. I ask You to help me guard my heart each and every day while I focus on You.

DAY 12
WHAT IMMORALITY ACTUALLY BRINGS
Scripture Reading: Proverbs 5:1-14

Only about 3 percent of Americans wait until marriage to have sex. While this is an alarming statistic, a survey done in 9 Southern Baptist Churches in Texas is even more frightening. In that survey, it was discovered that only 20 percent of church members aged 25 or younger were married without ever having premarital sex.[8] Only 20 percent. How sad. That means out of every 10 kids involved in church, 8 of them will fall to immorality. What a sobering thought. It's no wonder this passage of Scripture spends so much time warning young people of the allurement and dangers of sexual sin.

The writer first focuses on immorality's charm. The reason for the above statistics is not that those people necessarily sought out immorality. In fact, many of them probably never dreamed of doing such a thing. But immorality enticed them. The Bible describes the lips of immorality as "honeycomb," and "smoother than oil." Those words carry the idea of "flattering", "enticing," and "deceitful." In all honesty, immorality is attractive. If you are a human being then at one point or another you will experience the attraction it offers. You can be a good christian with high moral standards

---

[8] 4 Cool Statistics About Abstinence in the USA." WTMorg Social Network and Dating Site for Those Who Wait 4 Cool Statistics About Abstinence in the USA Comments. N.p., n.d. Web. 01 June 2017.

40

and still fall to the allurement of sexual sin. I love what John Butler has to say about this passage. "Evil is always very attractive in its solicitation. The harlot can charm one right out of their morals."[9] Don't ever think you are "too good" to fall into sexual sin.

Next, in verses 9-14, the Bible talks about the destruction that immorality always brings. Read through these carefully. May the damage it brings encourage us to stay far away from it!

In verse 9, we see that sexual sin always brings dishonor. Don't throw away your honor! God's Word is also describing how immorality will also fill your years with cruelty. You are too young and have too much life ahead of you to literally fill your years with cruelty. Sin is a cruel master.

In verse 10, the Bible says immorality will cost you money! No one likes to throw away their money. Immorality is expensive. It often costs people their jobs, lawsuits, child support, and more. Save your money and stay away from immorality!

It is no secret that immoral actions often lead to diseases. That's exactly what verse 11 is talking about. While staying pure will definitely help your physical health, it will also lead to a healthy marriage later on. It is a proven fact that waiting until marriage greatly improves your relationship with your spouse.

[9]Butler, John G. *Proverbs to Song of Solomon*. Clinton, IA: LBC Publications, 2013. Print.

Verse 11 also talks about the heartache immorality brings when it uses the phrase "mourn at the last." While sexual sin promises pleasure, it actually brings heartache. I know someone who once went too far with his girlfriend. While he repented and got things right with God, his heart ached for years afterward. Protect your heart from such emotional damage!

Regret is sure to follow immorality. Sexual sin will have you reciting verse 12 as it says, "How have I hated instruction, and my heart despised reproof." A regretful life is a sad life. Don't live it!

Lastly, verse 14 warns us that immorality will bring embarrassment. We like to sin without anyone knowing. And in the moment of temptation, the thought of getting caught never crosses our minds. But God sees our sin, and before long, others will as well. Mathew Poole says, " I, who designed and expected to enjoy my lusts with secrecy and impunity, am now made a public example and shameful spectacle to all men."[10] Avoid the embarrassment of sexual sin!

Understanding the charm of immorality and destruction of immorality should help us to avoid immorality all together. Let's follow the instruction of verses 7-8 by remembering and listening to the Word of God and staying as far away from sexual sin as possible!

----

[10]Poole, Matthew, "Commentary on Proverbs 5:14". Matthew Poole's English Annotations on the Holy Bible. http://www.studylight.org/commentaries/mpc/ proverbs-5.html. 1685.

- How has immorality been enticing to you?
- Can you see through the charm of sexual sin now that you know the destruction it brings?
- Are there any relationships you need to end or avoid after reading this passage?

Prayer: Lord, thank You for Your Word that helps me see the truth of immorality. Although it isn't easy, help me to do everything I can to stay away from the very temptation of sexual sin. Remind me of the dangers of it and the blessings that come with being pure.

DAY 13
ARE YOU AN ANT OR A SLUGGARD?
Scripture Reading: Proverbs 6:6-11

My former boss once told me a story about his middle aged nephew who lived in his mother's basement. I'm sure many of you could think of someone you know who still lives with his mom and dad. And in some cases, rightfully so. But this wasn't the case with this man. My boss informed me that the reason his nephew still lived with his parents was because he was lazy. In fact, he was so lazy that he wouldn't even go upstairs. Having a bathroom down there, all he needed was someone to bring him food. So for years his mother brought him food every day and he never left the basement. The last I heard of this man, he had gained so much weight that he literally couldn't go up the stairs if he tried. He couldn't fit! This man took laziness to another level.

In case this story isn't enough to motivate you to not be lazy, we're going to look at some biblical truths about how to develop a good work ethic and avoid the sad life of a lazy person.

The Bible begins by giving us the example of the ant. The ant is the most industrious insect God created. It's even busier than the bee! Have you ever took time to watch ants? If you do, you will often seem them carrying stuff to and from their nest. Often carrying something that is much bigger than them. God's Word tells us to follow the ant's example when it comes to working. How can we do that?

First of all, we can follow the ant's example by disciplining ourselves to work. The Bible says in verse 7 that the ant "has no guide, overseer, or ruler." In other words, ants have no one telling them to work. They simply do it on their own. I had a coworker who would only work when the boss was around. If the boss wasn't there that day, you could count on him to do absolutely nothing. Don't be that kind of employee. Don't make your boss, your parents, or teachers tell you to work. It should be something that you do on our own. Develop a work ethic that doesn't need a boss to make you work.

Secondly, we can follow the ant's example by working for a future harvest. Working isn't always fun. If it was, there would be a lot less grown men living in their parents' basements. The Bible doesn't say that the ant works for fun, but that it works for a harvest (verse 8). The ant, like every other creature, wants food and shelter. Therefore it works to have those things. Because of their hard work, when the harvest comes, they will have food and shelter! Just as a farmer works all spring and summer long to have a harvest in the fall, we too, should work to receive a harvest. What do you want the harvest to bring you: A car, college, a home? Then work for it!

In verses 9-11, we see the work ethic of the ant compared to the laziness of the sluggard. It's a fairly simple comparison as the ant works and the sluggard doesn't. As a result, the ant has plenty: plenty of food, plenty of shelter. It lacks nothing. On the other hand, the sluggard is poor. The Bible promises that poverty will accompany those who are lazy.

When I was engaged to my wife, I was working one job and barely making any money. I knew that in order to provide a place to live and food for my soon to be bride, I needed another job. Working two jobs wasn't the most pleasant thing in the world, but it was well worth the harvest that it brought. Without that job we either wouldn't have gotten married or ended up in a family members basement. I didn't like those two options, so I worked, and I'm so glad I did! Not only did I get to marry my wife and have a nice place to live, I was able to be proud of my work in providing for my family. The harvest is always worth the work!

- Are you more like the ant or the sluggard?
- What changes do you need to make in your work ethic?
- What do you want the harvest to bring you?

Prayer: Lord, thank You for creating me to work and accomplish things. I ask that You help me to develop a work ethic that pleases You. For I know that if I am faithful to work, You will be faithful to provide.

DAY 14
HOW DISGUSTING ARE YOU?
Scripture Reading: Proverbs 6:16-19

I once had a job as a maintenance man at Autumn Ridge Apartments in Sterling Heights, Michigan. Although it was a fairly easy job, there where plenty of disgusting tasks that I was assigned to. One of those tasks was cleaning out an elderly couple's apartment after they had moved out. Doesn't sound too bad. After all, I did this kind of thing all the time. But when I walked through the doors of that vacant apartment I began to gag and almost vomited. I soon learned that this couple was too old and feeble to take care of themselves. The only bathroom in the apartment was upstairs and they couldn't walk up the stairs. This often led to them using the bathroom on the carpet, and there were plenty of horrifying stains to prove it. And guess who got to tear up the carpet and throw it in the dumpster? Yours truly. Out of all the things I've ever done, that was probably the most repulsive.

In Proverbs 6:16 the word "abomination" means something that is morally disgusting. Is there anything in your life that is morally disgusting to God? Sure, it may be accepted in our culture. Everyone else may think it's no big deal. But is God pleased with it? Or are there things in your life that are repulsive in the eyes of a holy God? Today, we are going to look at seven things that God hates.

Pride is the first thing mentioned in this passage. Those who are prideful have a high opinion of themselves and a low opinion of others. They believe they are better than most people. As a sports fan, there are some athletes that I cannot stand simply because they are oozing with pride. What about you? What's your view of yourself? How do you view others? Instead of being prideful, we should realize that we are no better than anyone else. And without God, we are absolutely nothing.

The second sin this passage mentions is a lying tongue. In our culture lying has become the norm. Many television shows and movies depict lying as funny and no big deal. That couldn't be further from the truth. When we are dishonest, God is disgusted by our sin. Don't follow the culture's acceptance of lying! Tell the truth in all situations!

"Hands that shed innocent blood" is the next repulsive sin mentioned in verse 17. When I read this passage I couldn't help but think of abortion. If a fetus has blood, which it does, then isn't abortion the shedding of innocent blood? Oh how disgusting abortion is in the eyes of God. Not only abortion, but all murder. And while this should come as no surprise to anyone, it should be very alarming to see how God puts pride and lying in the same category as murder.

The fourth sin mentioned in this passage is a "heart that deviseth wicked imaginations." This is referring to evil thoughts. Every sin ever committed was first conceived in the mind. We know that our mind is a powerful thing. What we allow our mind to dwell on often determines our actions. While many believe bad thoughts are no big deal as long as you don't put them into action, God's Word says otherwise. Bad thoughts are morally disgusting to God. Did you realize that the music you listen to, the

48

things you watch, and the books you read all contribute to the thoughts you have? That is why it's so important to be careful with our entertainment choices. Guard your mind! Fill your mind with wholesome, God honoring thoughts!

"Feet that be swift in running to mischief" is the fifth sin God hates. This refers to the readiness and willingness to do evil. There are people all over the world who are constantly looking for something bad to get involved in. Don't be like those people and don't hang around those people.

The sixth sin is a false witness. This refers to those who, in a courtroom setting, spread lies. These lies are either to cover up their own wrongdoings or to hurt others. We see this in politics all the time. God is not a fan of "fake news." Those who take part in this sin will one day have to give an account to the Almighty God for their actions.

Finally, God hates the sin of sowing "discord among the brethren." I've seen first hand how spreading rumors, gossiping, or talking about someone behind their back can cause unimaginable problems among christians. No doubt, there have been countless churches split because of this very sin. God is disgusted by this kind of behavior and we should be too. How sad it is when christians tear down each other by using the devil's tactics. Are you causing problems in your church or youth group?

If we were to be honest with ourselves, there are probably a few of these sins that we struggle with. Instead of trying to hide our sin, let's own up to it and seek God's help in overcoming it. While God does indeed hate sin, He also loves to forgive. Perhaps you need to ask God to forgive you of your sin and to help you do right.

- Do any of these 7 sins have a place in your life?
- What do you need to do in order to overcome these sins?
- Do you realize the difference between how culture perceives these sins and how God does?

Prayer: God, help me to see sin for what it really is. Give me an understanding of how morally disgusting it is in Your eyes. While I live in a culture where sin is everywhere, help me to be different and live right.

DAY 15
PARENTS AREN'T SO BAD
Scripture Reading: Proverbs 6:20-23

Today's culture often depicts parents as dumb, old fashioned, and unfair. In fact, I bet in this past week you have seen a show on television where some teenager rebelled against his parents. It's the "cool" thing to do. No one goes to school talking to his friends about how great his parents are or how they are always right. The truth is, Satan doesn't want you to respect your parents. He's using culture to try and drive you away from the godly influence they can have on your life. Why would he do that? Because he knows that if you follow the instruction of godly parents, your life will be on the right track.

The reason why many teenagers rebel against their parents is because they don't like being told what to do. They have a "know it all" attitude. While it's tempting to have that mindset, it can be very dangerous. Teenagers are young, inexperienced, have an underdeveloped brain, and often throw caution into the wind. Truthfully, it would be foolish for young people to go through life without the instruction of godly parents or role models.

Verse 20 says to "keep thy father's commandments." That verse means to listen to them and apply them. In other words, when your parents give you rules, obey them. When they give you advice, take it. When they tell you to do something, do it. When they give you instruction on various issues, apply it. It's simple! The Bible also says to "forsake not the law of thy mother." This carries the idea of being faithful to listening and obeying your parents. It's not enough to obey them once a week. It's not enough to listen to their counsel every now and then. It's not enough to obey their rules most of the time. God tells us to be faithful in listening to and obeying our parents every single day.

The Bible tells us to "bind them continually" and to "tie them about thy neck." Do any of you have jewelry that you wear all the time? When I got married my wife gave me a ring. Now I'm not a big jewelry guy. I usually don't like to wear rings, necklaces, etc. But my wedding ring is different. I love it! Not only do I think it looks cool, but it's also a symbol of commitment my spouse and I have made to each other. The phrase "Tie them about thy neck" carries the idea of wearing a precious necklace. We are to view the instruction of godly parents or role models as precious jewelry that we wouldn't leave the house without. Don't go anywhere without your parent's or role model's instruction being on the forefront of your mind!

What happens when we listen, apply, and obey the instruction of our parents or role models? Verse 22 gives us a few advantages that are life changing! First of all, it will lead us. Young people, be honest with yourselves. You need leading. And God has placed godly people in your life to help lead you down the right path to a good life. The Bible also says that following our parents instruction will keep us. As we mentioned before, there is safety in wisdom. There is safety in following the rules and instructions set up by godly parents. So many young people have gotten into serious trouble and even ruined their lives because they neglected the teaching of their parents. Don't let that be you! Lastly, Scripture teaches us that listening to our parents will "talk with thee." That means it will give good counsel. On a daily basis it will help you make good decisions that will lead you down the right path.

Read verse 23 and notice the phrase "Reproofs of instruction are the way of life." Do you want the best life possible? Then follow instruction! Satan wants you to think that obeying your parents is lame—that you are missing out. But that couldn't be further from the truth! Do you want to get the most joy and fulfillment out of life? Then do what this passage says and listen to your parents!

Before we close I want to mention one more thing. I understand that many of you reading this do not have Christian parents. In such cases, you should still obey them and follow their rules (as long is it doesn't contradict the Word of God). Then, seek out a godly adult who you can look up to and get counsel and advice from. I promise they will be more than happy to help.

- How do you view the instruction of your parents?
- What changes do you need to make in order to follow the instruction of your parents?
- If you don't have godly parents, who is the godly role model you get counsel and advice from?

Prayer: Lord, thank You for placing godly parents or role models in my life. Help me to listen to their instruction and apply it. May following their biblical wisdom be a priority in my life!

DAY 16
AFFECTION FOR THE RIGHT THINGS
Scripture Reading: Proverbs 7

Alexey Bykov is a Russian man who went through extraordinary lengths to propose to his girlfriend. In fact, he claims that he loved her so much that he wanted her to realize how empty her life would be without him. Therefore, he hired a movie director, stuntmen, make-up artists, and a script writer to help him stage his own death. So while his girlfriend was on her way to meet him, she saw a trauma scene unfold on the highway. His car was horribly wrecked, ambulances were there, and her boyfriend's lifeless body was laying on the ground covered in blood. When she got out of her car the acting paramedic gave her the worst news of her life. "The love of your life is dead" he said. After a few seconds of sobbing, her boyfriend pops up, grabs a balloon and asked her to marry him. Surprisingly, she said yes.

This Russian man showed his love for his girlfriend in a strange way. His affection led him to do a drastic thing. What do you have affection for? We live in a culture where sexual sin is running rampant. Pornography is so easily accessible. Impure relationships are the norm. Texting, snapchat, and social media in general are often used for inappropriate conversations and pictures. So how can a young person overcome such temptations? By having affection for the right thing! Let us look at how sexual sin attacks us and how we can overcome it.

This passage gives us a scenario of a young man who had no intention of partaking in sexual sin. But it sought him out, attacked him, and before long he gave in and did something that he would regret for the rest of his life. I'm afraid that story is very similar for a lot of young people. Many of whom had no intention of looking at pornography, going too far in his or her relationship, or using social media inappropriately. Satan is not new at this. He has a plan and scheme to ruin your life. And sexual sin is one of his favorite weapons.

There are 6 characteristics of sexual sin found in this passage:

1. Sexual sin thrives at night. Verse 9 says, "In twilight, in the evening, in the black and dark night." It's never a wise thing to be with someone of the opposite sex late at night. Nor is it wise to text, snapchat, watch tv, or be online late at night because you will tempted to do things you would never do in daytime when people are around.

2. Sexual sin allures with improper clothing. Guys, do your best to keep girls in immodest clothing out of your site. Ladies, do your best to dress modestly. Many young women have no idea how short shorts and low tops can cause young men to stumble. Don't be a tool satan uses to attack young men. What you wear matters!

3. Sexual sin starts small. Verse 13 says, "So she caught him, and kissed him." She didn't ask him to go all the way at the beginning. Just a simple kiss was all she wanted at first. Young people, Satan isn't going to tempt you to do something drastic. Instead,

he methodically tempts with small things that lead to big things. How many times has a simply kiss led to a huge mistake? Or how many times has a little google search led to a pornography addiction? Young people, guard against the small stuff!

4. Sexual sin offers pleasure. In verses 14-16 the harlot offers this innocent young man pleasure. Sin always promises pleasure. It's one of Satan's favorite lies. Don't believe it!

5. Sexual sin conceals the consequences. The harlot promises that there will be no consequences in verses 19-20. Satan wants you to believe that there are no consequences to sexual sin, only pleasure. But in reality, the consequences are far greater than the pleasure.

6. Sexual sin ruins lives. Notice verses 21-27. This young man's life would never be the same after this night. So many young people have ruined their lives because of sexual sin. While God offers forgiveness, we will still have to pay the consequences for the rest of our lives.

So how should we stay away from falling into the trap of sexual sin? By keeping our affection on the right things! Verse 2 says, "Keep my commandments, and live; and my law as the apple of thine eye." The phrase "Apple of thine eye" is used to express affection. In other words, we should have affection for the Word of God. It should be something very important to us and dear to our hearts. Think about this next time you are tempted with sexual sin. What do you love more God and His Word or the empty pleasure that sin offers? When we make God and His Word our deepest affection, it will be easier to say no.

-Can you see how Satan methodically works to destroy?
-What can you do to avoid temptation?
-How has God specifically spoken to your heart while reading this passage?

Prayer: Lord, first I want to thank You for Your forgiveness and mercy. So many times I have messed up. Thank You for being faithful and just to forgive me and restore me when I repent. Please help me to have affection for You and Your Word instead of the temporary pleasures of sin.

DAY 17
ROAD TO REWARD
Scripture Reading: Proverbs 8:1-21

During spring training the Detroit Tigers had a commercial that ended with the phrase "The Road Starts Here." It was implying that the road to a World Series Championship started in spring training. That's not the only time I've heard that phrase in regards to sports. Actually, it's used quite frequently. Every team desires to win their sports' ultimate prize. As a result, they do all they can to make sure they're on the right road to get there.

As a young person you are probably getting advice from all kinds of people about what you should do with your life, where you should go to college, who you should marry, and so on. And it seems like everyone has a different opinion about the path you should take. It can be a very frustrating time. After all, everyone wants a good life. You want to take the right path. But how will you know the right way?

This passage tells us that biblical wisdom is the road that leads to the best life. Verse 11 says, "For wisdom is better than rubies; and all things that may be desired are not to be compared to it." God's Word will lead you down the right path. It will save you from a lot of pain and heartache. And it will also give you a great reward later on in life. Sadly, however, many young people don't care about what the Bible has to say. They have their own ideas of what is best. They do not understand that God's plan for their life is far greater than anything they could imagine.

Because we don't have time to focus on every verse in this passage, we're going to focus on verses 20-21. Verse 20 says, "I will lead in the way of righteousness." That carries the idea of leading us to do what is right. As a young person there are many difficult and confusing situations you may find yourself in. Knowing what to do is not always easy. That's why it's critical that we allow God's Word to lead us to know and do what is right. I love Proverbs 8:17 when it says, "Those that seek me early shall find me." That's talking about youth. Young people, what an opportunity you have to seek God and His wisdom while you're young! If you do, God will lead you down the right road before you make a wrong turn.

Verse 21 speaks of the rewards of going down the road of righteousness. The Bible uses the words "substance" and "treasure" to define what lies ahead for those who go down wisdom's path. There are countless blessings awaiting those who listen and apply God's Word to their hearts and lives. While life on this earth will never be perfect, God will bless you if you do things His way. The obedient life is an abundant life. John 10:10 says, "The thief cometh not, but for to steal, and to kill, and to destroy: I am come that they might have life, and that they might have it more abundantly." Jesus wants to give you the best life possible! That starts by applying biblical wisdom to your life.

Some of you may be in a stage of life where you have some major decisions to make and you have no clue what to do. Will you simply allow God to lead you down the path of righteousness? Will you study His Word and apply it to your life every day? Will you commit your life to doing what God wants you to do instead of what your family and friends want you to do? While it's not always easy, it's worth it, because God's path is a road to reward.

- What other things did God speak to your heart about that we're not mentioned in this devotion?
- Who or what are you allowing to lead you: Biblical wisdom, friends, family, culture?
- What actions, if any, need to take place for you to get back on the path of wisdom?

Prayer: Lord, Thank You for being a God who wants the very best for my life. I pray that You would give me a tender heart that will listen and obey the truths of Scripture. May You make the road of righteousness clear to me and help me to follow it every day.

DAY 18
THE HUNT FOR WISDOM
Scripture Reading: Proverbs 8:22-36

Note: while this devotion will focus on verses 33-36, I encourage you to read verses 22-32 in light of the fact that wisdom is portrayed as Christ.

One of my favorite things to do is hunt. I was blessed to grow up in a family that hunts and I remember being so excited when I could finally go hunting with my dad. One of the most exciting moments of my life was when I killed my first deer. But it didn't come easy. In fact, I spent many hours in the woods before I was finally successful. It took a lot of watching and waiting. But the moment I got one, it made all the watching, waiting, and freezing worth it!

The Bible says that blessed is the person who watches and waits for wisdom. Verse 34 carries the idea of one watching and waiting for school to start. It describes someone who cannot wait to learn more wisdom. My guess is that most of you don't show up at school an hour early waiting for the doors to open so you can run to your classroom and learn. I know I wasn't like that. But that's the kind of eagerness and excitement we should have to learn God's Word.

Why should we be excited to learn biblical wisdom? Because wisdom offers two great things that nothing else can. Verse 35 says, "Whoso findeth me findeth life." Butler comments regarding this verse, "Real wisdom is where life is. Life is not in

Budweiser or other intoxicating drinks. That's the
devil's lie. Life is in Divine wisdom."[11] Those who
seek God's Word and apply it will receive eternal life
in Heaven and an abundant life on earth. The best
life isn't found in riches, fame, popularity, marrying the
right person, etc. The best life is found in the Word of
God!

Wisdom also offers God's favor on our lives.
Notice what the Bible says in verse 35: "whoso findeth
me findeth life, and shall obtain favour of the Lord."
What could be more fulfilling than pleasing our
Heavenly Father? When we seek His wisdom and do
it, we are honoring our Lord and His favor will be on
our life.

If wisdom offers life and favor, why aren't we more
excited to learn from God's Word? Why don't we
show up to Sunday school excited and eager to learn
from the Scriptures? Why are we so lackadaisical
when it comes to hearing the preaching and teaching
of God's Word?

A couple years ago a youtube video was published
of Chinese Christians receiving their very first Bible.
When the luggage arrived full of Bibles, these
Christians ran and tore the suitcase open as they laid
their hands on a their own Bible for the very first time.
They began to hug and kiss their Bible as tears rolled
down their faces. It's un-telling how long they had
waited for their own copy of God's Word. How many
of us have Bibles that we never open just sitting in our

[11]Butler, John G. *Proverbs to Song of Solomon*. Clinton, IA:
LBC Publications, 2013. Print.

room? How many of us have the opportunity to learn from God's Word every day and don't take advantage of it while thousands would do anything to learn from it? How many of us have lost our excitement for the Word of God?

When you go deer hunting, you watch and wait for any and every opportunity to shoot a deer. Are you hunting for wisdom? Are you watching and waiting for every opportunity you have to learn from God's Word? Are you going to church, doing your devotions, going to Bible studies eager to learn? Oh What amazing things God's Word would do in our lives if we would seek it out with excitement!

-When was the last time you were excited to learn from the Word of God?
-Do you show up to church excited to hear and learn the God's Word?
-What else did you learn from this passage of Scripture?

Prayer: Lord, it's so easy for me to get excited about things like sports, movies, music, and other things. Will You ignite in me a passion for your Word? Will You help me to be passionate and excited about learning from the Bible? Thank You, Lord, for Your Word that is filled with truth and life changing power!

DAY 19
ARE YOU ON THE RIGHT DIET?
Scripture Reading: Proverbs 9:1-6

At 39 years old, Tom Brady won his fifth Super Bowl making him the most accomplished quarterback in NFL history. One of the most remarkable things about this achievement is that he shows no signs of slowing down. Brady will be 40 years old before he starts his 18th season for the New England Patriots. An age that is rarely seen in major sports, especially in a physically demanding sport such as football. But Brady is in great shape and seems like he could play for another 5 years. What makes Tom Brady so much different than everyone else? Why is he aging so much better than every other quarterback to ever play the game? He believes it's because of his intense diet.

80% of what Tom Brady eats is vegetables. He doesn't consume white sugar, white flour, caffeine, dairy, tomatoes, peppers, mushrooms, eggplants, gluten, or table salt. He eats some fruit, whole grains, brown rice, quinoa, millet, beans, and lean meat such as steak, duck, chicken and wild salmon. And of course everything is organic.[12]

While eating like that may seem a bit crazy, it works. Because Brady eats like no one else, he plays

---

[12]Tamarkin, Sally. "How Would You Eat Tom Brady's Diet?" *BuzzFeed*. N.p., n.d. Web. 25 July 2017.

like no else. That is one of the things that makes him so great.

The same thing is true when it comes to wisdom. The Bible says that wisdom provides a place of safety and security, a firm foundation on which to build our lives. Remember the story of the wise man who built his house upon the rock? That passage is referring to those who build their life around the truths of Scripture. Proverbs 9:2-3 depicts wisdom as preparing a great meal and sending out an invitation for all to come and eat. But what kind of meal is it?

It's not a literal meal. Instead, it's an illustration portraying wisdom as food; something that is much more beneficial than actual food. While a literal meal provides energy for the body, wisdom provides a formula for life which gives security, safety, peace, and happiness. In other words, biblical wisdom offers you the very best life possible.

Not only is it a great meal, but it's for everyone! Look at verses 3-5. This invitation was a public one. It wasn't just for the high in society. It wasn't only for those who were poor and needed a meal. It was literally for every single person. But there was one catch: in order to accept the meal of wisdom, they must reject the foolish ways of this world (verse 6).

Not only does Tom Brady eat certain foods, he must also reject certain foods. It would do him no good to eat all of that healthy grub for dinner only to eat a gallon of ice cream for dessert. Young people, the same applies to us. It does us no good to learn biblical wisdom if we do not reject the sinful teachings and practices of this world.

Satan is making his best effort to teach young people lies such as evolution, sex before marriage is cool, drugs and alcohol aren't that bad, authority is stupid, money is everything, etc. I obviously didn't mention them all but I think you get the point. So what meal will you choose? Will you choose that of biblical wisdom or will you fill your life with what the world has to offer? Remember, Tom Brady eats like no one else so he can play like no one else. If you go against the grain and live like no one else (according to God's wisdom), then later you will live like no one else (happy, blessed, safe, etc.).

-What is your diet? Are you feeding yourself God's Word or worldly wisdom?
-Is there anything in your "diet" that you need to get rid of (forsake)?
-Will you allow the benefits of doing God's Word motivate you to live right?

Prayer: Lord, we live in a culture that is constantly pushing worldly wisdom down our throats. It would be so easy for me to give in. Especially when it seems as though everyone around me is buying into it. Will You help me to see the benefit of knowing and doing Your Word? I ask that You would give me the ability and the boldness to live right. May You use my different lifestyle to be a light to my friends, classmates, teammates, and family.

DAY 20
ARE YOU COACHABLE?
Scripture Reading: Proverbs 9:7-12

In a 1992 NFL game the Chicago Bears were playing the Minnesota Vikings. The Bears were up 20-0 when their quarterback, Jim Harbaugh, called an audible at the line of scrimmage only to throw an interception that was returned for a touchdown. Bears, coach Mike Ditka, was furious as he started yelling at Harbaugh as soon as he got to the sideline. In the post game interview Harbaugh owned his mistake and said that Coach Ditka wouldn't let him call an audible anymore. This may seem a bit mean spirited, but in reality, coach Ditka was simply trying to correct his quarterback's mistakes, and it was up to Harbaugh to learn from them and improve as a player.

If you have ever played sports you probably know exactly what it's like to have a coach give you constructive criticism. That's the coach's job. To correct your mistakes and help you improve. However, there are many athletes who think they are "too good" to be coached or "too perfect" to ever make a mistake. I love the following quote from former University of Tennessee Women's Basketball Coach Pat Summit: "How can you improve if you are never wrong? If you don't admit a mistake and take responsibility for it, you're bound to make the same one again."[13]

Coaches are there to correct our mistakes. It's up to us to listen to them so that we can get better. In a similar way, we have godly people in our lives who correct us with biblical wisdom when we do wrong. They are kind of like "biblical coaches" who correct our mistakes and lead us to do right. How we respond to these "coaches" says an awful lot about us.

The Bible says in verse 8 that if you correct a scorner he will "hate thee." How do you respond to correction? What is your attitude when your pastor, youth pastor, or parents inform you that you're doing something wrong? Do you get angry and upset? If so, then it could very well mean that you are a scorner. And by the way, a scorner is one who mocks biblical wisdom. You don't want to be a scorner.

The Bible also says that when you correct a wise man he will "love thee." What a difference! Instead of being upset and insulted, the wise person is grateful for the correction because he wants to be the best christian he can possibly be. Are you thankful when godly people in your life confront you of your sin and give you biblical advice for how to live your life? If not, you should be! The Bible calls these people wise.

---

[13]Walls, Jerry L., and Gregory Bassham. Basketball and Philosophy: Thinking outside the Paint. Lexington, KY: U of Kentucky, 2008. Print.

I was listening to sports radio the other day when I heard a story from former New England Patriots offensive coordinator, Charlie Weis. Weis recalled a practice in which Tom Brady made a mistake and he absolutely chewed Brady out. In that moment, Tom Brady didn't argue, make excuses, or even yell back. He simply said, "My bad coach, it won't happen again." This kind of coachable attitude is what made Tom Brady so great.

What about you? Are you coachable? When confronted from the Scripture do you correct your mistakes or do you get mad and rebel? It's one or the other. The Bible says in verse 12 that the decision is up to us and the consequences of that decision will follow us. Will you be coachable?

-How do you respond to biblical correction?
-What godly figure/figures in your life can you count on to give you sound biblical advice?
-What changes do you need to make in order to be coachable?

Prayer: Heavenly Father, thank You for the godly people You have placed in my life to help me live and do right. I pray that You would give me a coachable attitude that will listen to loving correction. May I aspire to be the best christian I can possibly be!

DAY 21
DO YOU MAKE YOUR PARENTS PROUD?
Scripture Reading: Proverbs 10

Note: While we will only be studying verse 1 today, I encourage you to read the whole chapter underlining or highlighting the verses the speak to your heart. This will be especially helpful since we will be in Proverbs 10 for the next couple days.

As a kid, there was rarely anything I enjoyed more than hearing my parents say they were proud of me. I loved my mom and dad and wanted to make them proud. Knowing they were happy with me gave me a great sense of joy! On the other hand, knowing they were upset with me broke my heart. I hated it. I imagine that a lot of you are just like me. You want to make your parents proud. You want them to beam with joy when they talk about you to their friends. You want them to be thrilled with the person you have become. Thankfully, the Bible gives us a simple formula for how to make that happen!

Verse 1 says, "A wise son maketh a glad father." This verse isn't just talking about sons and fathers, but kids and parents. The key to making your parents proud is being wise. You may be thinking, "I'm so young, how in the world am I supposed to be wise?" While our culture has the perception that only old people are wise, that doesn't have to be the case. Wisdom is found in the Word of God. As a young person you can be just as wise as anyone if you learn, listen, and apply the Word of God to your life.

For example: think of everything you have learned in these devotions the past 20 days. In only 9 chapters, we have learned a ton about how to live a life based on the foundation of God's Word. If you do the things God's Word has taught you, you will no doubt make your parents proud!

On the contrary, the Bible says that a "foolish son is the heaviness of his mother." I had the opportunity to preach at a youth camp a couple years ago. When I arrived, I knew absolutely no one. Thankfully, there was an older lady who went out of her way to talk to me and make me feel comfortable. In fact, she was very encouraging throughout the week. One afternoon as the campers were preparing for their canoe trip, she began to tell me a funny story about her son. We laughed for a few seconds and then I asked her "What's your son up to now?" Immediately her laughter turned into tears. Long story short, her son wasn't right with God and making foolish decisions that broke his mother's heart.

If I were to ask your parents how their children were doing what would their response be? Would they be beaming with pride? Or would tears begin to role down their faces? Many young people have broken their parents' hearts because they have rejected the teaching of God's Word and have made foolish decisions instead. I don't want that to be me. I don't want that to be you. With the Lord's help will you make a decision to live a life based on biblical wisdom that will make your parents proud?

Maybe some of you have already made some decisions that broke your parents' hearts. That doesn't mean it has to be like that for the rest of your life. God offers forgiveness and the chances are your parents will too! Ask God and your parents to forgive you and give you another chance to make them proud!

-Is there anything in your life that your parents aren't proud of?
-Are you making biblical decisions or foolish ones?
-Is there anything that you need to apologize to your parents for?

Prayer: God, thank You for Your Word that contains the answers to everything in life. While many people my age are making foolish decisions that are breaking their parents' hearts, help me to live in a way that brings pride to my parents instead of shame.

DAY 22
THE POWER OF THE TONGUE
Scripture Reading: Proverbs 10:11,14,20,21

The Bible has plenty to say about our tongue and how we use it. Words are obviously a huge part of our lives! Whether in school, work, church, friendships, or relationships, we speak or listen the majority of the time. In James 3:3-5, Scripture speaks of the incredible power of the tongue: "Behold, we put bits in the horses' mouths, that they may obey us; and we turn about their whole body. Behold also the ships, which though they be so great, and are driven of fierce winds, yet are they turned about with a very small helm, whithersoever the governor listeth. Even so the tongue is a little member, and boasteth great things. Behold, how great a matter a little fire kindleth!" James compares our tongue to a tiny bit in a horses mouth that controls the whole body of the horse. He also uses the comparison of a small helm used to guide a large ship. This passage tells us that our words have tremendous power!

Today, we are going to look at four verses that contrast godly words with wicked words. I pray that we would understand the power our words carry and dedicate them to be used for good!

Verse 11 describes the words of a godly person as a "well of life." Commenting on this verse, John Gill says these words are "like a fountain of living water, continually running and flowing with water, wholesome, reviving, and refreshing."[14] When the words that come out of your mouth are pure, wholesome, and encouraging, they will give life to others. In a world where young people are so damaged by hurtful words, your words can be refreshing to them! Wouldn't it be awesome if your words had a positive impact on others? They can!

However, the Bible says that "violence covereth the mouth of the wicked." This means that only evil and hurtful words come out the mouth of the wicked. Are your words refreshing or hurtful?

Verse 14 talks about how wise men lay up knowledge. They do not talk all of the time trying to make themselves look smart. They simply, and quietly, learn and obtain wisdom and speak when it is the right time and place. However, the foolish mouth wastes no time blabbing things. They rashly and carelessly say what comes to their mind and it usually ends up hurting others and causing problems. Have you ever hurt someone with a careless word? I'm sure we all have. May God help us to be a quiet learner instead of a babbler!

"Choice silver." That is the phrase verse 20 uses to describe the words of the godly. The Bible is very specific. It doesn't just say "silver," but "choice silver." There's a big difference there! Choice silver is free from dross (it has no crummy stuff in it), pure, consistent, and of great worth and value. When your

---

[14]Gill, John. "Commentary on Proverbs 10:11". "The New John Gill Exposition of the Entire Bible". http://www.studylight.org/commentaries/geb/proverbs-10.html. 1999.

words are godly, they are of incredible worth! Do your words match the criteria of "choice silver?"

The Bible also says in verse 20 that "the heart of the wicked is of little worth." While godly words have incredible value, the heart of the wicked, from which flow his words, is worthless and good for nothing. Do you want your words to be valuable or worthless?

Lastly, verse 21 says "the lips of the righteous feed many." This carries the idea of nourishing as well as guiding. Like a shepherd who guides his flock, godly words will impact many lives for God's glory! On the contrary, while righteous words lead many to safety, wicked words lead many to destruction.[15] Your words will have an impact either way. Make sure the impact is a good one!

Don't forget about what James said about our tongue. It is a powerful thing! Your words make a monumental impact on others. It is up to you how you use that influence. Will you surrender your words to God and allow them to be wholesome, pure, and uplifting? Or will you allow you words to have a negative influence by talking bad about others, swearing, or talking inappropriately?

- Are you words having a positive or negative influence on others?
- Now that you know your words are powerful, how will you use them for good?

---

[15]Barnes, Albert. "Commentary on Proverbs 10:21". "Barnes' Notes on the New Testament". http://www.studylight.org/commentaries/bnb/proverbs-10.html. 1870.

- What changes do you need to make in the words you speak?

Prayer: Lord, I pray that You would help me to realize the impact of my words. Help me to speak godly, wholesome, and uplifting words. Also, help me to not say hurtful or wicked words that can so easily come out of my mouth. May You use my words for Your glory!

DAY 23
ARE YOU HATING OR LOVING?
Scripture Reading: Proverbs 10:12

In case you haven't noticed, we are an imperfect people. I imagine that all of us have been hurt in someway or another by the ones we love. What's even more sad is that too often people never forgive each other when these hurtful things take place. Stuff like this happens all the time in high school. Someone gets upset at his friend for something, he then proceed to tell everyone in the school what his friend did, and then holds a grudge with all of his might. And of course, they can no longer be friends. Although this is very childish, it happens in the adult world as well. Too many relationships have been ruined because of hate. However, the Bible tells us to forgive and forget. And we should! After all, didn't Jesus forgive and forget our sin?

The Bible says that "hatred stirreth up strife." The phrase "stirreth up" means "to uncover." In high school there was a girl in my class who was accused of making out with some boy. The next day, a few kids kept bringing it up all day. Through subtle jokes, looks, and laughs, they were "uncovering" her sin. The Bible calls this hate. While what she did was indeed wrong, it was a hateful thing to uncover her sin in hopes to embarrass her and cause problems.

The phrase "hatred stirreth up strife," can also apply to those who like to cause drama. I am 100 percent certain you know someone who loves drama. They love the opportunity to stir up drama and cause problems. A couple of years ago we were playing basketball after church when out of nowhere a young lady came storming through the parking lot wanting to fight my wife all because of something she "thought" my wife said. Thankfully, my wife wasn't there, because honestly, she didn't stand a chance in that fight. Don't be the person who seeks to cause drama, spread rumors, and keeps bringing up other people's sins. According to the Bible, this is a form of hate!

Instead, the Bible calls us to love. The Scripture says, "But love covered all sins." This means to look passed, to forgive, and to forget the sins of those we love. Perhaps you have had someone very close to you hurt you in some way. Instead of keeping his sin at the forefront of your mind and never letting him live it down, you are to forgive and forget his sin. To act as if it never happened. While that will not be easy, it's wise! And it's in your best interest as well. Because not only will the one who hurt you be happy, but you will be freed from the hate you once harbored in your heart.

Who is it in your life that has hurt you and done you wrong? A parent? A friend? Someone in authority? Will you hold a grudge? Will you keep uncovering his sin without any indication of forgiveness? Or will you forgive and forget and treat that person like nothing ever happened? The Bible tells us to do the latter.

- Who has done you wrong?
- Are you forgiving them or holding it against them?
- How can you be like Jesus by "covering up" their sins?

Prayer: Lord, I ask that You would help me to forgive and forget. Help me to understand that no one is perfect. When people mistreat me, help me not to hold it against them, but to love them instead!

DAY 24
GOD CARES ABOUT HONESTY
Scripture Reading: Proverbs 11:1,3

Note: While we will only be studying verse 1 and 3 today, I encourage you to read the whole chapter underlining or highlighting the verses the speak to your heart. This will be especially helpful since we will be in Proverbs 11 for the next couple of days.

Working in the apartment industry for a couple years, I got to see some of the shady, dishonest deeds that took place. I heard of people who bought refrigerators with company money and then sold them out of their garage. Another instant involved this one manager who claimed she had around 20 vacant apartments. But in reality, she was renting them out for cash and not telling corporate so she could pocket the money herself. I heard stories like this all the time. And every story ended with "they got caught."

This passage is talking about honesty in business. Have you ever been to a candy store? You get a bag and go through the store filling it with the goods of your choice. Once you are done, they put the bag on the scale and weigh it. You're charged per ounce for the candy. A "false balance" would be if they made the scale weigh more than what it actually did in order to charge you more money. It's dishonest, and in reality, stealing.

While this practice probably doesn't take place at candy stores, although it might, it happens all the time in the business world. Whether it's stealing refrigerators or putting extra weight on the candy scale, some people will do anything to make a little extra money. The Bible calls this dishonest and it's an "abomination" to the Lord. In other words, God hates it!

Verse 3 says that the "perverseness of transgressors shall destroy them." This means that the sinful ways, words, and actions will eventually be their ruin. If you pay attention to the news, you will eventually see a story where a business or person is in trouble for being dishonest. For example, a few years ago the news came out that Joe Paterno's assistant football coach, Jerry Sandusky, sexually abused children. What made matters even worse is that Paterno knew about it and hid the facts in order to keep his football program from being penalized. While he got away with it for years, the news eventually came out and Joe Paterno went from being one of the greatest football coaches ever, to a dishonest person who contributed to some disgusting deeds.

Listen to this quote by Joe Paterno days after the disgraceful news came out: "My name, I have spent my whole life trying to make that name mean something. And now it's gone." Can you see how the sinful, dishonest ways of Joe Paterno lead to his destruction? This is exactly what verse 3 is talking about!

On the other hand, the beginning of verse 3 says, "The integrity of the upright shall guide them." God promises to lead and bless those who are honest in business. Simply put, integrity leads to a good life. Dishonesty leads to destruction.

At some point, you will be pressured to take the dishonest way. Whether it's cheating in school or dishonestly making a couple extra bucks at work, the temptation will be there. But don't forget what the Bible says! Integrity will be your guide to making a nice living. Dishonesty will only lead to your downfall.

- Are you honest at school or work?
- Can you think of any examples where integrity helped someone?
- Can you think of an example where dishonesty ruined someone's life?
- What changes do you need to make in your life in order to be a man or woman of integrity?

Prayer: Heavenly Father, I live in a world where many people are trying to take the dishonest way to success. Help me remember that dishonesty will only bring destruction and integrity will lead to a better life. Show me areas in my life that need to be changed so that I can be the person You want me to be.

DAY 25
SEEK WISE COUNSEL
Scripture Reading: Proverbs 11:14

In October of 1962, Premier Nikita Khrushchev delivered nuclear missiles to Cuba and President John F. Kennedy demanded them to be removed. This resulted in the United States being on the verge of a nuclear war with the Soviet Union. As you could imagine, tensions were high during this dangerous time and President Kennedy had pivotal decisions to make.

Before making any decisions, President Kennedy did something very wise. He called three former US Presidents to get their advice. Herbert Hoover (who faced the great depression), Harry Truman (who ended World War II), and Dwight Eisenhower (who served as a commander in Europe) all gave great insight to the President. Kennedy took their advice and made a balance course of action that ended the crises and a nuclear war was avoided.

Whether he knew it or not, President Kennedy took advice from the Word of God and sought a multitude of wise counselors which led to safety. Had he not asked for advice, he could have made poor decisions that could have changed our nation forever. To be honest, it would have been foolish to take action without consulting wise people first.

Many young people are not fond of seeking advice from adults older and wiser. They would rather do their own thing, believing they know what's best.

That's a dangerous way to live life. The Bible says, "Where no counsel is the people fall." Living life without seeking advice from godly people is a life destined to fail.

In every life-changing decision, and there are many of them, we should seek advice from the godly people we look up to. Whether it's a decision about college, a career, dating, marriage, family, and everything in between, we should surround ourselves with godly people who will give us godly advice for those decisions.

On January 20, 2017, President Donald Trump was sworn into the oval office with no political experience whatsoever. While many thought this would be a huge mistake, others said as long as he surrounds himself with wise people he would do just fine. The Bible says "In the multitude of counsellors there is safety." That's true for President Trump, for us, and for everyone!

- Who are the godly people in your life you seek for advice?
- What decisions do you have coming up in the next few years that require wise counsel?

Prayer: Lord, thank You for the godly people You have placed in my life. Help me to seek their advice on important decisions. Also, help me to trust in what they have to say, even when it's difficult to hear.

DAY 26
WISDOM WINS
Scripture Reading: Proverbs 11:30

Have you ever been fishing? Whether you have or not, I imagine you understand how it works. Fisherman put bait or a lure on a hook in hopes to attract fish. Once the fish bites, they set the hook and reel it in. Have you ever tried to catch a fish without bait? If so, then you probably weren't very successful. Fishermen use bait or lures to attract fish so they can catch them. For some people, fishing isn't just something to do on a nice weekend, it's their livelihood. Such was the case for disciples Andrew, Peter, James, and John. In fact, they were fishing when Jesus called to them saying, "Follow me, I will make you fishers of men." Jesus invited them to follow him and make winning souls their business.

The Bible says, "He that winneth souls is wise." It's a very wise thing to lead others into a relationship with Jesus Christ. After all, eternity is real. Heaven or Hell will be the destination of every soul. We could spend our lives doing a lot of "good things," but nothing is more important, more rewarding, than leading people to Jesus.

The Hebrew word for the phrase "he that winneth" means "to take or catch." It carries the idea of a fowler. A fowler was someone who made a living from catching birds and selling them. Just like the fowler makes it his life business to catch birds, we should make it our life business to win souls to the Lord![16]

Not only is it wise to win souls, but wisdom is often the "bait" that lures them in. You see so many people in this world who have devoted their lives to making money, to sinful pleasures (sex, drugs, alcohol, etc.), to making a name for themselves, and so on. And you know what all these people have in common? Deep down they are miserable. They soon find out that what they wanted so badly doesn't satisfy. So when they see someone who is living the truth's of God's Word (wisdom), and see how different his life is and how happy he is, it draws them to that person. When Biblical wisdom is lived out, people will be drawn to it. In other words, living right gives you a great opportunity to lead others to Christ!

Young people, it's wise to win souls and it takes wisdom to win souls. Devote your life to the most important business in the world. There's no business like soul business! So be a light in this dark world and tell everyone you can about the wonderful, merciful, life changing love of Jesus!

- How devoted are you to winning souls?
- When was the last time you prayed for someone who wasn't saved?
- When was the last time you told someone about Jesus?

---

[16]Poole, Matthew, "Commentary on Proverbs 11:30". Matthew Poole's English Annotations on the Holy Bible. http://www.studylight.org/commentaries/mpc/ proverbs-11.html. 1685.

Prayer: Dear Lord, help me to be a great soul winner. I ask that You would forgive me for all of the opportunities I have wasted. I pray that You would put in my heart a love and passion for those who aren't saved. May my life be a testimony of how You saved me, changed me, and gave me true happiness.

DAY 27
The Fruits of Righteousness
Scripture Reading: Proverbs 12:2,3,7

Note: While we will only be studying a few verses today, I encourage you to read the whole chapter underlining or highlighting the verses the speak to your heart. This will be especially helpful since we will be in Proverbs 12 for the next couple of days.

A couple of days before I quit my job as a maintenance man, my boss called me into his office for a talk. He was a Christian man and simply wanted to thank me for my time there as well as ask what my plans were as I went into full time ministry. Before I left he told me that he had seen God's favor in my life. I was curious and asked him to give an example. He then replied, "When you asked for time off to preach at that camp. My boss told me that if you left, you wouldn't have a job when you came back. And here you are." Long story short, they didn't fire me. I am certain it was because of God's favor on my life!

In Proverbs 12 we learn that righteousness produces God's favor. Verse 2 says, "A good man obtaineth favour of the Lord." First of all, it's important to note that we can only be "good" with God's help. We must rely on Him to make us into the man or woman He wants us to be. On our own, we are nothing but sinners. It takes God's power to help us do right. That being said, we have a choice. We can either live a life of sin on our own or we can count on God's help everyday to live a righteous life in everything we do. I recommend the latter because there's nothing like having God's favor resting on your life!

When we first found out my wife was expecting, I couldn't help but want a boy. My sister-in-law said, "It will probably be a boy because everything always works out for Trav." We laughed and then later that night I began to really think about that statement. I reflected on all the things that had happened in my life the past two years. I had married my wonderful wife, got the job of my dreams, bought a lovely home, and now a child was on the way! It really did seem like everything was working out for me. I knew it was nothing but God's favor on my life!

In verse 3 we see that righteousness provides a strong foundation. Read these words closely. "A man shall not be established by wickedness: but the root of the righteous shall not be moved." Sinful living makes a crummy foundation to build your life on. It will leave your life in an absolute mess! On the other hand, righteousness is a foundation that will survive even the strongest of storms. Take Chick-fil-A for example, they hold to their christian values and refuse to work on Sundays. To the world, this seems like a foolish business decision. But in reality, they are more successful in six days than most businesses are in seven. Their foundation is paying off! Point being, build your life, family, and business on righteousness and you will never go wrong!

Lastly, we see that righteousness produces a blessed family. Proverbs 12:7 says, "The wicked are overthrown, and are not: but the house of the righteous shall stand." God does not only bless the righteous person, but the entire family of the righteous person. While you may not have a family of your own yet, one day you will. While that can be very exciting, it also comes with a lot of responsibility. Here's a sobering thought: your spouse and children will be affected by the way you live your life. If you live a sinful life, they will have to pay for some of the consequences. If you live a righteous life, they will be blessed! Live a life of righteousness now so that your family will be blessed later!

- Is your life on a wicked foundation or a righteous one?
- Do you know anyone who has God's favor on his life? If so, follow that person's godly example!
- Do you know anyone who built his life on a sinful foundation? How's that working out for him?

Prayer: Lord, thank You giving me the power and ability to do right. I ask that You would help me to build my life on a righteous foundation. Thank You in advance for the favor You will show on my behalf.

DAY 28
DON'T TRAP YOURSELF
Scripture Reading: Proverbs 12:13

At a Bank of America in Corpus Christi, Texas, a man had accidentally trapped himself inside the A.T.M. while working on the machine. For three hours this man was locked inside a tiny space. What made matters even worse was that no one could hear him and he didn't have his phone with him. He did, however, have a pen and paper which he used to write a note and slip it through the machine's receipt slot to everyone who used the A.T.M. Thankfully, someone finally took the note seriously and got help.[17]

I imagine that was a rough three hours for that man. Three hours that he will never forget nor repeat. You only get locked in an A.T.M. once before you learn your lesson! In Proverbs 12:13 the Bible compares wicked words to a snare. Something which hunters would use to trap animals. One thing is certain, no one wants to be trapped!

I have never trapped animals before, but I've seen people do it on TV. And while I may not know what kind of animal it is or the worth of it's fur, I do know this: it never ends well for the animal. They end up mangled, bloody, and dead.

---

[17]"Man Trapped Inside Texas A.T.M. for 3 Hours Is Rescued by Police." *The New York Times*, The New York Times, 13 July 2017, www.nytimes.com/2017/07/13/us/man-trapped-atm-machine.html.

Isn't it ironic that Satan uses lies and evil words as a form of temptation to get people out of trouble when in reality it does the opposite? This world is so accustomed to lying and hurtful words that it's rarely seen as a big deal. It's become the norm for people to use wicked words. And while these people think they're getting out of trouble, they're really just taking one step closer to stepping in a trap!

The Bible says, "The wicked is snared by the transgression of his lips." How many times have the lies of politicians been exposed and led to their ruin? How many times has a nasty gossip come back to bite the gossip spreader? How often have hurtful words led to the punishment of the one who spoke them? In other words, your sinful words such as lies, gossip, and hurtful remarks are really a trap. When you speak them, you are setting up a trap in which you will assuredly fall into.

I have seen many people speak wicked words that came back to bite them. The truth will always come to the surface and the words you say will always be revealed. Like toothpaste, once you squeeze it out, you can't put it back in. So it is with our words. Once spoken, they cannot be unspoken.

Young person, don't set traps for yourself to fall into. Don't mangle your relationships with hurtful words and lying lips. Don't try to get out of trouble by lying. That it will only make matters worse. Instead, tell the truth! The last part of verse 13 says, "But the just shall come out of trouble." While the wicked get

snared by their evil words, those who avoid evil
speaking will avoid trouble.

- How will this Biblical truth change the way you
  speak?
- Can you think of any times where your wicked
  words got you in trouble?
- What ways can we avoid trouble altogether?

**Prayer: Lord, this culture is filled with people who
use their words wickedly. While it would be so
easy to do the same, help me to be different. Help
me to avoid the trap that evil words set and to
speak wholesome, truthful words that will keep
me out of trouble.**

CONCLUSION

I realize we only covered the first twelve chapters of Proverbs. I encourage you to read and study the rest on your own. Don't let your devotional time stop here! I hope and pray that tomorrow you will pick up your Bible, turn to Proverbs 13, and spend time with God through Bible reading and prayer. My goal for this book is to get young people in the Word of God and to keep them in the Word of God. Make spending time in Scripture a priority in your life. Below are a list of tips that will help you in your daily devotional life.

1.   Do you devotions at the same time every day. This will help develop a habit.
2.   Read carefully in order to understand. It's better to read one verse and understand it than to read a whole book and not remember what you read.
3.   Write in a journal as you read. Write the things God speaks to your heart about as well as your prayers.
4.   Underline or highlight verses that speak to your heart.
5.   Don't give up! You will be tempted to quit. But if you keep reading every day you will eventually get to the place where you love it and can't go without it!

BIBLIOGRAPHY

Barnes, Albert. "Barnes' Notes on the New Testament". http://www.studylight.org/ commentaries/bnb/proverbs-10.html. 1870.

Butler, John G. *Proverbs to Song of Solomon*. Clinton, IA: LBC Publications, 2013.   Print.

Elliot, Elisabeth. Shadow of the Almighty: The Life & Testament of Jim Elliot. San   Francisco: Harper & Row, 1989. Print.

Gill, John. "The New John Gill Exposition of the Entire Bible". http://www.studylight.org/ commentaries/geb/proverbs-10.html. 1999.

"Overview - English Annotations on the Holy Bible." *StudyLight.org*. N.p., n.d. Web. 05   May 2017.

Poole, Matthew. Matthew Poole's English Annotations on the Holy Bible. http://   www.studylight.org/ commentaries/mpc/proverbs-5.html. 1685.

StudyLight.org, www.studylight.org/pastoral-resources/illustration-archive/search.cgi? query=SAFETY&x=0&y=0.

Tamarkin, Sally. "How Would You Eat Tom Brady's Diet?" *BuzzFeed*. N.p., n.d. Web. 25   July 2017.

The New York Times, The New York Times, 13 July 2017, www.nytimes.com/ 2017/07/13/us/man-trapped-atm-machine.html.

Walls, Jerry L., and Gregory Bassham. Basketball and Philosophy: Thinking outside the Paint. Lexington, KY: U of Kentucky, 2008. Print.

49887970R00057

Made in the USA
Middletown, DE
24 October 2017